Tricky Little Hippo

Jane Bowring
illustrated by Nina Rycroft

Flying Frog Publishing

For Anna — J.B.
For Charlie — N.R.

an imprint of Scholastic Australia Pty Ltd
PO Box 579 Gosford NSW 2250 ABN 11 000 614 577
www.scholastic.com.au

This edition published by
Flying Frog Publishing
Lutherville, MD 21093

Made in China

Two little hippopotamuses stared at the water.
They were counting. "Nine, ten, eleven, twelve..."

A little way down the river,
the big hippos rumbled and grumbled,
but the little hippos took no notice.

"Thirteen, fourteen, fifteen..."

Above them, a bird squawked and flapped its wings,
but the little hippos didn't lose count.

"Sixteen, sevent...OOOOH!"

There was a splash
as a roly-poly little hippo
burst out of the water.

"How many did I do?" cried Holly.
Water sprayed from her ears
as they popped up straight.

"Seventeen," said Heath.
"Oh," said Holly. "Is that all?"

It was two better than Heath,
but Honey had stayed under the water
for *twenty-one* whole seconds.

“Let’s play a different game,” said Holly.

“Chasing in the mud!” yelled Honey, and the three little hippos raced off to the mud hole just beyond the reeds.

They squealed and they squelched,
and they rolled and they belched,
and the mud squished through their toes
as they chased each other
through the slippy, sloppy mud.

Heath caught Holly,
and Honey caught Holly,

and Holly caught Honey,
and Heath caught Honey,

but nobody came even close
to catching Heath.

The three little hippos played
and played until the sun began to go down.
When their mothers came to get them,
they couldn't tell which little hippo was which.

As the frogs began to croak
their evening song,
Holly's friend Egret
flew down from a tree.

"Did you have fun today?" said Egret.

"Yes," said Holly, but then she sighed.

"What is it, little one?" said Egret.

"Well," said Holly, "Honey
was best at staying underwater,
and Heath was best at chasing.
I want to be best at something, too."

“You are best at something,”
said Egret.

“I am?” said Holly.

“What will we play today?” asked Holly the next morning.

“Hide and seek,” said Heath. “I’ll be it.”

Heath covered his eyes and began to count.

Honey swam off and hid behind
a clump of water reeds.
She stayed very, very still.

Holly crouched behind her mother
who was dozing on the river bank.

"Ready or not, here I come!"
cried Heath.

Heath looked all around him.
He looked at the big hippos
resting in the shallows,
their heads pillowed on each other's backs.

He looked at the water reeds,
long and green at the water's edge.

And then he looked at Holly's mother,
snorting and snuffling on the river bank.

Peeking up behind her back he saw two little ears.

"Found you! Found you, Holly!" he cried.

"Let's play a different game," said Holly.

"I know," said Heath. "Who can open their mouth the widest!"

Honey went first.
She opened her mouth very wide.

Holly went next and
she opened her mouth even wider.

But then Heath opened
his mouth so wide
that his teeth glinted
in the sunlight.

As the frogs began to croak their evening song,
Holly's friend Egret flew down from a tree.

"Did you have fun today?" said Egret.

"Oh, yes," said Holly, "but...
Honey was best at hiding
and Heath was best at opening his mouth.
I want to be best at something, too."

"You are best at something," said Egret.

"I am?" said Holly.

The next day Honey said, “Let’s play who can stay underwater the longest.”

Holly didn’t want to.
She was sure Honey would win again.

But then she saw a dark shape walking on the bottom of the river and she changed her mind.

Honey went first and she stayed under for twenty-two seconds. Heath went second and he stayed under for twenty-three seconds.

And then it was Holly's turn.
She took a huge gulp of air
and sank beneath the water.

“One, two, three...”
Honey and Heath began to count.

“Eight, nine, ten…”
They were counting so carefully
they didn’t see Holly walk along the riverbed
and go around behind them!

"Fifteen, sixteen, seventeen…"

Heath and Honey were counting so carefully they didn't see Holly watching them from the reeds.

"Twenty-one, twenty-two..."

Holly would have to come up soon.

Egret flapped his wings
and flew down onto Honey's back,
but the two little hippos didn't lose count.

"Twenty-six, twenty-seven..."

Heath and Honey were getting worried now.
No little hippo had ever stayed under this long.
They stared hard at the water.

They were staring so hard they didn't notice
the little eyes, ears, and nose
gliding silently toward them.

They were staring so hard that
when a roly-poly shape burst out
of the water behind them bellowing,

"Tricked you! Tricked you!"

they all bellyflopped into the water.

When Holly looked at her friends' astonished faces,
the grin on her face was so huge
that her teeth glinted in the sunlight.

"I'm the best at being tricky!

I'm the best at being tricky!"

she roared.

"You are indeed," said Egret,
shaking the water
from his feathers.
"You are the
trickiest little hippo."